Bulletproof Habits for Success

*Learn how successful
people achieve self-realization*

OSWALD CHAPMAN

Table of Contents

Introduction

You want to become successful. You can feel that there is more to life than what you are presently enduring. It has crossed your mind more than once that maybe you are doing things the wrong way. You need a new approach to ensure you give life your best shot at becoming one of the individuals that history can never forget. You can make your indelible mark on the line of history as a successful person by trying some Success Rituals.

You are right about needing an approach to attain success. Success Rituals shares insight into steps that successful individuals conduct daily and some that you might want to implement in your life.

The natural order of life is that things go through stages. Take, for instance, the process that it takes to create a child. In the womb, there are a series of steps, and after birth, there is another. Nevertheless, each child develops at a different pace. Some kids walk or talk before what is considered the "expected time" for them to do so. Success Rituals are processes that individuals endure to become prosperous. Achievements during the stages are different for everyone. However, there are similarities in each stage of the Success Rituals, just as how there are similarities in the stages to produce a child, but the outcome differs.

Success Rituals have certain fundamentals that every successful individual had to do, and some which they had to learn how to overcome. Likewise, you must decide without any form of doubt that you too will have to work hard and overcome whatever obstacles you will encounter on your journey.

You might be the one that will develop before the expected time frame for one to become a success. Do not delay for another minute. It is time to discover empowering Success Rituals, which will assist you in conquering your fears and progress on your destined journey of prosperity.

Chapter 1

Success Rituals Fundamentals

D o not be scared of the word rituals. Ritual is just a synonym of the word habit. We all know that our thoughts and actions over a period of time will determine how we progress in life. Positive rituals yield positive results, and negative rituals will produce undesirable results. We have many rags to riches story, and you might be a rags story awaiting the right rituals to change your situation to riches. You will never know until you examine your life and make the necessary modifications. It is time to change your perception about rituals.

Learn To Discover Your Talents

You will find individuals with similar Success Rituals, but they all produce different results. This is because everyone has different opportunities and how we react to situations is different. Notably, persons will have similar talent, but each talent comes with a unique ability. If you do not discover the uniqueness that comes with your talent, you might never truly stand out from the others that are in the exact field as you are. If you cannot produce extraordinary results, then your advancement will be either mediocre or below average. Mediocre and below average results will never give you the title of a successful person.

You will only discover the uniqueness that comes with your talent after you have started using your talent. Let us take a look at some Success Rituals Fundamentals that you must ensure you develop. Build your rock-solid Success Rituals starting with those listed on the ladder below:

The first step on the Success Rituals Fundamentals is to believe in YOU. If you do not believe in yourself, you will never really discover your true potentials. Apart from finding what hidden treasures of skills you have buried within, is knowing, how and when you are at your best. Some people will tell you that they think better having a hot cup of coffee. Some after they take a shower or go for a jog, then ideas will start to overflow in their head. Think back to the time you were able to unravel your best idea. What were you doing at the time that happened and where were you when that happened?

If possible, go back to the exact location and repeat the same action of what you were doing, and try to discover more great ideas. You will need to purchase a notebook. You must always have something close by to write down your thoughts. I am suggesting that you get a notebook because ideas will pop in your head at various hours of the day or night. For example, you might find yourself suddenly awakened by an idea that popped into your head, and you want to write it down immediately. Moreover, trust me, this does happen in the middle of the night when you start developing yourself. Electronic devices take some time to get booted up, and you might lose your thought. However, if you have a notebook, you just quickly fetch your notebook and make jottings, then in the morning, you could type and save your concepts in whatever storage software you use. No matter how brilliant you are, you will not be adept at retaining all the images in your head. The thought that you will forget, if you do not jot it down, might be the very idea which is your ticket to get on the success train.

Developing the healthy habit of jotting down your ideas also allows you to analyze better your plans, and to be able to group or tweak them. That is progress, and you will feel good at what you have accomplished and be more motivated to put them into action.

You are elated now because you have chosen what you believe is the best idea and you are ready to put it into action. It will be at this moment that fear will opt to cripple your mind. Creating doubts about your idea and your ability to implement them successfully. If you do not believe in yourself, and if you have not entirely convinced yourself that this is your time. That you were born to make an indelible mark on the lines of history and you are feeling your greatness churning in the depths of your guts. That you cannot control it anymore and you need to find your best life. Then, I am afraid that you will only get stuck at jotting down great ideas and not knowing where those ideas would propel you on your predestined path of prosperity.

What is Fear?

Fear is the mastermind behind the death of many goals. We all know someone who is an "If I had." The "if I had" of life have many ideas and are always the first ones to tell you how to get things done even though they have never tried anything worth mentioning in their lives. Yes, they have all annoyed you and me at some point in time in life.

You might have even been an "if I had," but the fact that you are reading this book means there is hope for you. It is not too late for you to decide to change your situation in life.

 The only way to dispel you fear to take the necessary steps to set realistic goals and timelines for your concepts. The moment you decide to continue with your ideas, you will feel the power fear had over your mind slowly losing its grip. Fear will entirely lose its grip onyourmindwhenyourconcept becomes an action. So go ahead, even if you have to move with wobbling legs and shaking fingers, take your leap of faith.

The Fundamentals Ladder Of Success Rituals

Goal setting and time management are equally important on the Success Rituals fundamentals ladder. If you do not set targets with timelines, then you will have nothing to work towards and no achievements to look forward to celebrating. Setting goals is a medium that you can utilize to determine how close you are to achieving your plans. You have the ability to assess and make adjustment where necessary. It also assists in developing your skills set and discovering other talents that you were not aware that you possess.

Hard work and determination is what will transform your goals into reality. If you only work hard some of the times, then, you should anticipate the partial result. A mind that is determined is the fuel for hard work, and hard work keeps you determine. That is why both of them have to be used together consistently. It is impossible to achieve by having only one of the two. Think of determination and hard work that they are Siamese twins. They should always be joined, and it must be challenging to identify one from the other. Muhammad Ali has a quote that has an element of humor to it, but it also clearly depicts what you have to do if you want to achieve your goals.

"The best way to make your dreams come true is to wake up."
– Muhammad Ali

You have to wake up, be determined, and work hard.

Making improvements to your skills set and plans are another set of Siamese twins. If you improve on your skill sets, then you will discover other things that you can accomplish. You can gain success in other areas other than what you had made plans for initially. If you improve your strategies, then the possibility is that you will discover new abilities that you had no idea you had. The discovery of new skills can be by attempting to work on the improved areas of your plan yourself, or you can employ someone who completes the task in your revised proposal. If you hire an individual to perform the work, this is also a learning experience for you. You must always be aware of what is happening in whatever business transaction that you had initiated.

For me, the final Success Rituals Fundamentals is never fear failure. You will inevitably fail at some stage of your plan. Failure varies for different individuals. You might experience a massive failure, and have to start your journey entirely from the first step. Your failure might be minor, and with a few adjustment things can be back on the progress level. If you fear failure, you will not be able to recover from misfortunes. When you face failure, accept it, analyze what is the possible cause or causes, and start strategizing immediately to correct, as well as, prevent it from reoccurring, your fears will begin to diminish.

Success Rituals are crucial because we all need them to become successful. If we try to skip a step, then, we can be sure of a definite fall. The fall will be in the form of failing to achieve our goals. Take things step by step while you discover yourself and find your sole purposes for being awarded the gift of life. Learn to enjoy your roller coaster ride that life is guaranteed to take you on. No matter how badly you fail, you can always raise again if you work hard and if you are determined enough.

Chapter 2

Rituals Of Highly Successful Individuals

A re you wondering if Success Rituals are real? Well, this is what this section will clarify for you. I will be sharing with you rituals of high success and how it will help you get ahead of the regular folks in life. Take a look at the morning, evening, and business rituals of some highly successful individuals below:

Morning Rituals Of Eleven Highly Successful Individuals

Mark Zuckerberg (Co-founder and CEO of Facebook) – I am wondering have you noticed that the man who has his name enlisted on almost all the billionaire list that you can grace your eyes on seems to only have gray T-shirts. These gray T-shirts are not a uniform for his company. The wearing of only gray T-shirts by Mark Zuckerberg is a deliberate act. This is his way of saving time in the mornings. Even after he is sometimes up all nights discussing with an employee, you can still find Mark Zuckerberg up by the clock strikes six in the morning. Without out having to worry what clothing to wear for the day Mark Zuckerberg grabs his outfit, which is usually his gray T-shirt and then he is off to work at his office early in the morning.

Padmasree Warrior (CEO NextEV, U.S.) – A true warrior of time and rising early in the mornings to complete most of her task is Padmasree Warrior. While the night shadows cover the land, and with the twinkling of the stars which probably reminds her that she is among the most successful women; at 4:30 in the mornings Padmasree Warrior is up and working. Padmasree Warrior starts the day by going through her emails for approximately an hour. Then, she ensures she is kept informed about current affairs by reading the newspaper. After she reads the papers, then, it is time to ensure she remains fit and healthy, so she exercises. After her daily morning rituals, she is in her office by 8:30 in the mornings, ready to take on the challenges of a new workday.

Tim Cook (CEO, Apple) - Tim Cook not only enjoys his race of being up before the sun, but he is very proud of the fact that he is the first one to be at his company in the mornings and the last one to leave during the evenings. You can check for an email from Tim Cook as early as 3:45 in the morning; because that is when he gets up, and has become known for sending company emails at that time in the mornings. Tim Cook is one who ensures that he maintains his health; therefore, you can find him in the gym by five in the mornings.

Jack Dorsey (Co-founder, Twitter) – Tweet, tweet might be some of the twittering that Jack Dorsey hears at 5:30 in the morning when he is taking his six miles jog. Jack Dorsey also takes some time to meditate before he leaves for his run in the mornings.

Jack Ma (Founder, Alibaba Group) – As precious and swift as the wind is the commodity time. We cannot preserve time, and once past, we can either give thanks that we had used our time productively or live with the regrets of what we never used our time to accomplish. Knowing how precious time and his family are Jack Ma is up by the latest seven in the mornings. Jack Ma uses half an hour to complete some task, and then he ensures he spends some quality time with his family.

Kara Goldin (Founder & CEO, Hint Water) – It is time to take a hint. Most highly successful individuals are hitting the work button before the day is dawn, and Kara Goldin is among those who are doing so. Kara Golding day begins at 5:30 in the mornings. She peruses through her work calendar ensuring that she has no exigent meetings, and then she responds to emails. By 7:15, Kara Golding starts making her business calls, but not before she saturates her taste buds with a double latte, and she goes hiking with her husband.

David Cush (CEO, Virgin America) – Crunch time is at 4:15 in the mornings for David Cush. His fingers get busy to dial his associates' numbers who are on the East Coast, but not before he took some time to send his emails. Next, David Cush tunes his ears to Dallas Sports Radio, while his eyes are kept busy reading the newspaper. Then, he is off to the gym to ensure he keeps himself fit.

Dan Lee (Director, NextDesk) – It is time for a standing ovation because Dan Lee is up by the clock strikes 3:30 in the mornings. Dan Lee ensures that he is completely hydrated by drinking two litres of water, then, he also consumes two cups of coffee, and smooth things off with a smoothie. After Dan Lee hydrates his body, the next ninety minutes, he shares with his dog and reading. He reads for one hour and spends half an hour with his dog. Clearing his pours through perspiration, you can find Dan Lee in the gym from 5:15 – 6:15 in the mornings. When the clock ticks its way to 7:15 in the mornings, Dan Lee is already in his office, prepared to tackle the challenges of a new workday.

Sallie Krawcheck (Co-founder, CEO Ellevest) – It is the romancing of the mind with the lights dimmed or sometimes she seeks warmth from the fireplace, along with a hot cup of coffee and Sallie Krawcheck is ready to start her day at four in the mornings. While the lights might be dimmed in her home at four in the mornings Sallie Krawcheck is shining bright with ideas; because that is when her creative flair comes to light best.

Indra Nooyi (CEO, PepsiCo) – Popping as early as four in the mornings, is, Indra Nooyi. Her first task is ensuring that her plans are organized for the new day. Indra Nooyi is usually buzzing in her office by seven in the mornings.

Richard Branson (Founder & Chairman, Virgin Group) – He is certainly no virgin when it comes on to rising early. Not even the comfort of his private island can prevent him from pulling his curtains at 5:45 in the mornings to watch the rising of the sun. With a fantastic view of the rising sun, which comes with the opportunity to enjoy his fortune for another day, Richard Branson maintains his health by exercising and having a healthy breakfast. Then, he is off to work to ensure that he keeps making his billions.

Evening Rituals of Five Highly Successful Individuals

Bill Gates (CEO, Microsoft) – Bill Gates, dubbed the richest man in the world according to the Forbes Billionaires list. He reads for an hour almost every night before going to bed, no matter how late he gets home. One of the topics that have consistently sustained his reading habit is business-related issues, which Bill Gates uses to assess changes in the market (no surprise there right). He also read about politics and healthcare.

Joel Gascoigne (CEO, Buffer) – Walking for twenty minutes every evening. During his walk, Joel Gascoigne assesses his workday, analyses his greatest challenges, and then, he will slowly stop thinking about work when the shadow of tiredness takes over his body.

Arianna Huffington (Founder, Huffington Post) – At nights Arianna Huffington disconnects from the world of technology by turning off all her electronic devices. Then, she dissolves the stress from her workday by taking a hot bath. Arianna Huffington pulls the shutters on her day wearing her pajamas while she reads a physical book.

Kenneth Chenault (CEO, American Express) – Kenneth Chenault gets a head start to his days by setting goals for three things he wants to achieve every night before he goes to bed.

Oprah Winfrey (Business Woman and Media Mogul) – Oprah Winfrey ends her days just as how she starts them. She meditates twice per day, once in the mornings, and once in the evenings.

Business Rituals of Three Highly Successful Individuals

Amancio Ortega made it to Forbes Billionaire list as the second wealthiest person in the world. Amancio Ortega has five business rituals, which have guided him to success.

1. Speed is very important – Amancio Ortega took the retail industry by storm in 1975 when he founded his company named Zara. He used the tactic of ensuring that two times per week his store was restocked with the latest fashion. Another one of his strategies was getting new styles of clothing before his competitors, and the timely processing of customer's order within forty-eight hours.

Amancio Ortega plan worked; because he was able to satisfy his market better than his competitors, and have earned his organization the name of "Fast Fashion."

2. *Obsess with your customers need* - One of Amancio Ortega's motto is that the clients are the driven force behind a business, and should always be the central focus when designing your business. Customers need must also be your focal point when you are deciding on the operational systems that you will implement at your business, style of clothing that you will be selling, and any other activity that requires you interacting with your customers.

Being customer-focused meant that Amancio Ortega conducts consistent market research. His detailed analysis included him observing fashion blogs and directly garnering information from customers to keep a brief of the current trends in clothing.

3. *Being In Control Of Your Distribution Channels* - Amancio Ortega capitalizes on the cost-effectiveness of China clothing, but he also imports most of his products from other regions such as Morocco, Spain, and Portugal. Designing and sewing his products is one of medium Amancio Ortega swiftly meet the needs of his market by supplying them with the latest trends in fashion. He also utilizes a local network of sewing shops by having his designs cut, and treated in mills; then, they are sewed by the local sewing shops.

4. *Being Committed To Your Roots* – His ears buzzing from the ideas his employees' shares with him, as he sits, and work alongside them is the only office that Amancio Ortega has ever had. Amancio Ortega is from humble beginnings. He is the son of a housemaid, and railway worker, but his desire for a better life led him to stop attending school at the age of fourteen to start earning. Knowing what it is like to have nothing, Amancio Ortega never got himself an office, but instead, he takes a hand-on approach by working with his employees. Age has not slowed him down; because even at the age of eighty Amancio Ortega still goes to his office on most days.

5. *Continuous Innovations* – Complacency has no place among those who want to progress, and for those who want to remain successful. To become complacent is the biggest mistake you can make. You must have either grow or die attitude, and if you really want to be innovative, then, you cannot focus on the results.

Carlos Slim Helu has the tag of the fourth richest man in the world according to the Forbes Billionaire list. He has ten business rituals.

1. Making money in a downturn – Recessions cannot hinder Carlos Slim Helu from acquiring new businesses. His strategy is to take advantage of the companies that have been affected by the economic crisis, which has no significant financial problems. Some of the best companies are sold for half their values during a recession. Carlos Slim Helu was able to purchase the largest cement company world Cemex during the recession. Cemex currently has a net worth of approximately six billion.

2. *Simplicity in organizational structures is best* – Having a simple organizational structure with minimal hierarchical levels will allow

executives and lower line employees to be able to interact more frequently, sustain flexibility, and assist in quick decision making capability.

3. *Remain focused on innovation, growth, training, and quality*
– You must focus on innovation, growth, quality of products, training for employees and continually improve production processes. Analyze your organization based on global benchmarks, seek the most cost-effective means when possible, to reduce expense, and increase productivity as well as your competitiveness.

4. *You must live without fear and guilt* – Carlos Slim Helu believes fear is the worse weakness that men can have. Fear first weakens you, then, it impedes your action and eventually leads to depression. He believes that guilt is a terrible burden in people's lives, which influences the way one thinks and acts. Guilt and fear create difficulty for your present-day, and it is a hindrance for your future. To overcome both fear and guilt, one must have good sense, accept ourselves as we are, which means with whatever virtue, disappointments, and realities.

5. Making wise Invest in areas that customers find it difficult to avoid you – Carlos Slim Helu has made investments in a variety of industries. He has invested in the health sector, clothing industry, real estate, bakeries, telecommunication, academic institutions, and museums, just to name a few. Carlos Slim Helu many investments have allowed him to serve his customers daily through various mediums, making it impossible for them to conduct business, and not contributing to one of his establishments.

6. A good education will assist you in managing big a business better – Carlos Slim Helu believes that good decision making facilitates business success. You will be able to make better business decisions if you are armed with the information to do so, this comes from increasing your knowledge through education.

7. Try to be humble no matter your status – Carlos Slim Helu is aware that riches also come with a lot of responsibility; however, this has not prevented him from spending time with his family. He assigned two days out of each week for quality time with his family—one day for dinner with his sons, and another day for dinner with his twenty-three grandchildren. Carlos Slim Helu with all his billions, still drives himself to work, which is approximately an hour away from his home. He has also lived in the same home in the same neighborhood for over forty years.

8. *Prepare yourself for big opportunities* – Carlos Slim Helu believes one of the characteristics of becoming a successful entrepreneur is having the skill to identify great business opportunities and capitalize on your chances.

9. *Committing to the game* – Entrepreneurship and investing is like a game. If you want to succeed, then, it requires you to become committed to your entrepreneurial process and make decisions as if you are playing to win your entrepreneur and investing game to achieve success.

10. *Comprehending your business to the core* – Allegedly, Carlos Slim Helu controls approximately two hundred companies in different regions around the globe. He was able to accomplish this by ensuring that he comprehends his business to the core.

David Koch, the tenth billionaire on the Forbes Billionaires list.David Koch shared his five tips for you to start learning from those who are rich.

Below are David Koch's five tips:

1. Creating wealth through earnings and not saving– Successful individuals like David Koch continuous thoughts are how to earn big money and how to expand their potential profits. If you are not significantly increasing the sum of money that you have, then, there is a good chance that your savings will not make you a wealthy person.

2. Never be afraid to believe in your ability, and you should take smart risks – Many individuals refuse from taking risks because of the possibility exist that they might fail.

However, those who are successful know that you have to take risks both financially and in your personal life if you want to earn significant rewards. Successful individuals also accept that failure is the price you pay for your ultimate learning experiences, and you must develop the confidence to continue after you have failed.

3. Do not become emotionally attached to money– Prosperous individuals take a rational approach when they are building their wealth. They do not allow any negative emotions like anxiety, greed or regret to daunt their financial decisions, which have led to better chances for them to become successful.

4. Capitalize on all your opportunities– Successful individuals understand that every opportunity presents the possibility for them to achieve more, even if it is a partnership, project, or they are just negotiating to venture into a new business. They understand as well as appreciate the significance of networking. Successful individuals are always seeking new business ventures while capitalizing on their current assets to generate more income from different areas. Their positive attitude in every opportunity contributes to achievements in their business ventures and also to their wealth.

5. Understanding that your time does not equal money– Dispel the belief that the time you spent working hard will be equivalent to your level of success. Undoubtedly, successful individuals do work hard, but they have worked even smarter. It is not necessarily how hard you work but how smart are you working. Smart working means you strategize your time wisely, how you utilize your assets for them to assist you to increase your earnings. You should aspire to become an expert in your field, no matter what field of business you are working.

If your greatest desire is to disengage yourself from the grip of poverty, then you should adopt the rituals of the wealthy, be fearless, and have absolute confidence in your abilities. Believe that you deserve to have all the best that life has to offer.

Chapter 3

Empowering and Disempowering Rituals

I t is never too late to find new rituals or to improve on those you are currently practicing. We all have rituals, but the question that you need to ask yourself is: "Are my rituals empowering me or are they disempowering me?"

Make a list of the daily rituals that you have been doing over the past ten years. Analyze the outcome of each of these rituals. From your analyst of the habits that you have developed over time, how did they assist you in progressing to your desired has your goals? How daily routine affected your relationship with your family and your friends?

Suppose the answers to the above questions are ones, which clearly state that your habits have generated only a negative or mostly negative impact in your life. In that case, it is evident that you have disempowering rituals. It is time to change those disempowering rituals to empowering rituals.

The Power Of Your Thoughts

You have the power to change your thoughts, which will eventually influence your actions. Every one of your actions came about because of a thought that you had initiated. Whether that idea came about consciously or it was a subconscious thought. To create empowering rituals, you will have to learn how to reprogram your mind. To accomplish the reprogramming of your thoughts, you first have to find an empowering ritual that you will be used to replace the disempowering one.

Start your day with the right attitude, full of energy and refreshed with ideas. When your day gets off to a good start, you will be able to use your time more productively. We all have the same twenty-four hours in our day, but how we structure our activities for the day can make a lot of difference.

Let us take a look at some disempowering rituals that you might be practicing, and were not aware that they are not empowering you.

Nine Common Disempowering Rituals:

1. Getting out of bed long after the sun has comfortable settle itself in the sky and have provided great warmth for the Earth.

2. Lack of physical and mental exercise.

3. Unhealthy eating habits, which are leading to degenerative and other fatal health issues.

4. Your time is used for reading and watching the wrong kind of materials, which cannot assist you in achieving your ultimate goals.

5. The individuals that we interact with on a daily basis influence our thought process a lot more than we often realize. You will not find any successful people hanging out on the side of the street speaking to a group of individuals that only hangs

out on the street every day unless they are doing some kind of community outreach program. Gossiping on the telephone for hours would be considered unnecessary spending and valuable production time lost for a successful individual. If you keep spending most of your time with unproductive people, then, eventually you will become sterile. Make sure that you are not wearing the label of an unsuccessful person. Evaluate your acquaintances. Suppose you associate yourself with people who are thriving for success or who are already successful. In that case, you will be motivated to change your lifestyle to be more in line with the successful people whom you are now associating yourself.

Now, I am not saying that you should stop speaking to your friends if they are not productive. I am merely suggesting that you associate with them less and find more individuals that share similar success vision as you do. Successful people associate with other successful individuals.

6. Never making any plans for your day, you just go with the flow of any events. If you are not making plans to achieve, then you have quickly set yourself up for failure. So do not be surprised when you reap failure's results.

7. Poor time management. You might have made plans for your day, but you spent too much time conducting rituals that unproductive.

8. No form of academic improvement. While it is true that most of the world's wealthiest individuals might not have a master's degree, they continually educate themselves through daily reading of books or by watching various videos that will assist them in improving their skill sets.

9. The poor allocation of your finances is a disempowering ritual. Investing your money in things that cannot return a profit on your dollar will not let you become rich. It is nice to have a fancy car, beautiful clothes, and dine at the best restaurants, but these must only be a reward for the assets you have a mass through your hard work. Living like the rich and famous when your bank account, along with your wallet is still living in poor man's land, is a perfect example of you allocating your funds poorly. All the finer things of life that you want to enjoy now will still be available when you have mastered your success rituals, and you are financially capable of living life as a wealthy and famous individual.

Six Empowering Rituals

1. Exercise - your greatest wealth will always be your health. You should never sacrifice your health to achieve wealth. Your wealth will never truly restore your health, and you might not even live long enough to enjoy your success.

2. You must eat healthily and ensure you have adequate rest.

3. Get up early in the mornings. A great ritual that you must develop is to get out of bed early in the mornings. Creating a great head start to your day, and life begins with you getting up early.

4. Make plans in your journal for the following day before you go to your beds at nights and evaluate the activities of your day.

5. Find time to unwind and meditate. Spend some quality time with those you love.

6. Invest in yourself by increasing your knowledge about the field that you are in, and also learn how to spend your money wisely. Consistently, assess how your current asset can be allocated to allow you to earn more in different areas. Here is an excellent food for thought as you make plans to educate yourself:

"Formal education will make you a living; self-education will make you a fortune." Jim Rohn

What you do daily influences your life. If your rituals are disempowering, the, you will never yield positive or favorable results. On the contrary, if your rituals are empowering, then, you have a greater possibility of achieving some form of reward. Success starts in your mind, with the thoughts that you are forefront in your head because those thoughts are what will eventually empower your daily actions. Take a bit of advice from a woman who has dragged herself from the gutter of poverty to stand proudly among the wealthy, *Oprah Winfrey* stated:

"What we dwell on is who we become."

Chapter 4

Building Your OwnSuccess Rituals

After you have identified the rituals that you currently have, your next step is to assess what rituals you really need to practice. Then, it will be time to build your own success rituals.

You cannot build your own success rituals if you are not aware of what is that you need to be doing to ensure you become successful in your given field. If you actually want to become successful, then you must find out what rituals those who are successful in your given field have. Then, based on the information that you have garnered, you will build your own success rituals.

I believe it can be comfortably said that the majority of successful individuals are always out of bed before the sun rises. With that said, the first ritual that you should build is ensuring that you are also out of bed before the sun rises. A guru of productivity *Benjamin Franklin* stated:

"Early to bed, and early to rise makes a man healthy, wealthy, and wise."

Let us examine the benefits of rising early in the mornings:

1. There is just something about the dawn of a new day, before the sun makes it appear in the sky that fills your inner vessel with a lot of hope. Not even the polluted air, which is often found in urban regions, can eradicate that morning whiff of hope, even if you just open a window in your home to take a swift, deep breath of it.

2. A second benefit of rising early in the mornings is that you do not have a lethargic feeling, which typically comes with rising after the sun has risen.

3. You can get a lot more done during a day by having an early start.

4. The peacefulness of the morning gives you a chance to filter your thoughts more accurately and make better plans.

So you have mastered the task of getting up early, that is great; however, you must use your time productively. The best part of becoming wealthy is to know that you had done so while maintaining or with no comprise to your health.

To maintain or not to compromise your health, you will have to watch what you consume and ensure that you do at least half an hour of physical exercise each day or for a minimum of three days per week. Most of the successful individuals have incorporated exercise into their daily routine; therefore, the next morning ritual that you should develop is **exercise**.

Exercise is important to get your body in shape, but it also helps with developing a healthier mind for you to function better.

Exercising, as you know, is only a part of the process to keep healthy. You also have to eat healthy if you want the exercise to work efficiently.

Exercising and eating healthy is one way that you might cheat death to live a little longer so you can enjoy your wealth. So I am sure it is worth taking the shot at having a healthy lifestyle.

The aspiration to become the best at what you do is something that you must take into consideration when you are building your rituals. The great inventor and co-founder of Apple *Steve Jobs* said:

"Innovation distinguishes between a leader and a follower."

You should consistently brainstorm for ideas that will improve the plans you already have, and what will uniquely set you apart from others. Whoever is the best in the market will also amass the most success. Allocate time to cover all areas of your life. You need to find the time to exercise, meditate, make your schedule, and for work. You need time to have fun with your family and friends.

Start creating your own opportunities for success by ensuring you have some highly successful individuals in your circle. You already know that success is something that you have to work to obtain. So you have to not only think like those who are best but start talking, dressing and acting like you are the best too. That is a sure way of setting yourself up to become the best in your given field.

Chapter 5

Six Core Success Rituals

T here six core areas of success. Each area is important to create balance in your life. If you ignore one of the six core areas of success, then, you will not be able to function at your best. You will have a sense of lacking in your life and might even waste your time trying to fill the void with the wrong things.

The six core areas of success are listed below:

1. Physical Health – The emphasis can never be too much on how important it is to ensure you do all that is possible to sustain your physical health. It is quite logically that one of two things will occur if you do not maintain your physical health. It is either that you will have to spend your fortune on medications and doctors or you will be snatched too early death due to some form of health issue. Exercise, eat healthily, get adequate sleep, and drink a lot of water can assist in keeping you healthy.

2. Emotions – Your emotions affect your mind. If you are mentally unhealthy or unstable, then you cannot make objective decisions. A decision that is made when someone is emotionally unstable can wreak havoc on your life and has the potential to become very drastic, which we have all either heard, read or experienced personally.

All six core areas of success are correlated. Take, for example, if something happens to trigger your emotions in a negative way – you are feeling sad, or you might be angry - you can always exercise to calm yourself down. It is not only your negative emotions that you need to learn to control because if you are too excited or happy, but you can also make the wrong decision. For example, if you are overzealous, you might spend money on things which you do not need, and that money could have been invested in something that will increase your income. Life is about creating the right balance in everything you do.

3. Relationships – Your relationships can affect your health and your emotions. A toxic relationship will leave you with feelings of despair and anger. Unhappiness and rage can lead to depression. Depression will affect your progress, either by you losing time to work or by you making decisions, which will ultimately fail.

The benefit of good relationships will create a heaven for you on earth. The world in your eyes is at peace because your heart is full of love, and your mind will have its cover made from thoughts of joy. You will function better. You will be more eager to get up in the mornings because you are grateful for another day to be with the ones you love.

Examine your relationships, and see how they are impacting your life. If being around, someone makes you feel burdened, or you feel as if that person is pulling all your hope, and joy out of you, then that is a toxic connection. You need to disconnect from that person. Relationships that motivate you to become better or the ones that help your ideas sparkle are what you need in your life.

4. Career or Business – Observing the attitude people display at their place of work can always tell who loves their job from who do not. If you are not in the job or business which makes you feel that this is what you were born to do, then you might be in the wrong field. Your career or business must leave you feeling fulfill no matter the obstacles you face daily. The belief that the world could not exist without you doing that business or career find its resting place in your mind and heart. When in the right field, it will be easier to keep focus, and because of the passion you have for your career or business, failure cannot convince you to quit.

5. Finances – *"Money isn't the most important thing in life, but it's reasonably close to oxygen on the "gotta have it" scale." – Zig Ziglar*

Wealthy and happy is all of us heart's desire. However, if you want to be wealthy, it might take years of hard work to become rich, but it only takes a minute with a bad investment, which will result in you losing all your money. If you do not have money, it might make you unhappy because you cannot buy the things you need to support yourself or family. Not having money can also prevent you from investing in your career or business. However, you can have money and still not be happy, because there is unbalance in one of the other five core areas of success. Never spend money on things just because you want to impress others. That is definitely not a ritual of successful individuals. The wealthiest people live humble lives.

For example, Bill Gates has topped various billionaire lists for years. He can afford his own private jet. Bill Gates is known to comfortably sit in the economy class on airplanes when he is traveling.

Warren Buffet, with all his billions, is very much content in his home, which he bought for less than forty thousand dollars many years' ago. He also still makes his billion-dollar transaction discussion on his flip phone, which he has not replaced for any of the high-tech cellular phones that are available today.

They give back a portion of their wealth to various charitable organizations. Sometimes it is a charity that they have started or one that is already in operation. Even after death, the richest individuals are sharing their fortune. A lot of affluent individuals are willing their fortunate to charities. Melinda Gates and Bill Gates have a grant-making foundation where they give away billions to different charities around the world. They have also encouraged other billionaires to donate some of their fortunes to the less fortunate.

You must also adopt this principle of giving back to the less fortunate. Just as how you will start practicing the other success rituals, this is one habit you must also develop. Allocate whatever you can afford to charity now, and as your wealth increases, then, you increase the portion for charity as well.

6. Spirituality – No matter what your religious preference may be, spirituality is an important aspect of spiritual success.

Spirituality can be found all around you, from the time you spend in nature, to meditation, to your religious practices. Spirituality has the ability to ground you and keep you close to both your own personal feelings and help you work through anxiety and emotion, which will enable you to make sound and important judgments. Choose a spiritual ritual for yourself and stick with it each and every day.

Chapter 6

Morning Success Rituals

A vast amount of information was shared about morning success rituals throughout this book, and it is evident that you have to start your day right, to create the perfect momentum for the rest of the day.

1. Smile

Your first exercise routine should be a smile. A smile is free. It is the best cosmetic surgery, and it will help to relax you. Try smiling right now, and see if you do not feel an instant peace in your heart.

2. Show Gratitude

After you smile, then you should show gratitude to the world around you for the ability to experience a new day. Through meditation, you will hear your inner voice more distinctly. You will have the opportunity to search your soul and discover your most profound desires. Sometimes, if you listen keenly, you will begin to understand exactly what your path should be.

3. Drink More Water

Drink some water at least a liter to hydrate your body. Water helps with circulation, improves your skin tone, assists with weight loss, and the purification of your body. Water is the best drink to have. You must always consult your physician about things that will affect how your body functions before attempting to do them.

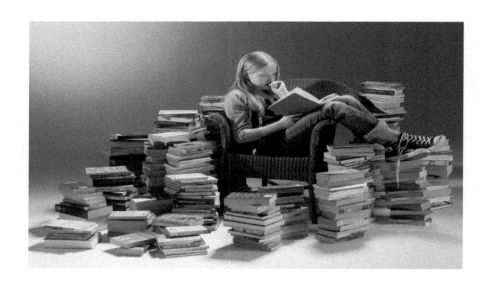

4. Positive Affirmation

You need positive affirmation. Motivational audios or books are a great source of motivation. After you meditate, then, you can listen or read from something from your favorite motivator. Positive affirmation is a must among your daily routine, and you have to learn to be your greatest source of inspiration. This will help to block all the negative voices, which will tell you that you do not have the ability to achieve.

Feeding your mind with positive food sets the tone for you to improve your knowledge. Take some time in the morning to read. Most of the knowledge you will acquire in life will come from your experiences and what you teach yourself.

5. Exercise

Next, you engage in some vigorous exercise. Go for a long walk or a run. Do some stretches or yoga. Get physically active.

By the time you have completed the above activities, you will feel fully rejuvenated and ready to face the new day. You can start with your most challenging task, and then work your way through the others. How you end, your day can impact how your day starts. Therefore, aim to end your day on a good note.

Your body needs time to unwind from the wear and tear of the workday. Take some time to relax in the evenings. Designate time for your family. Never neglect the one's you love in your pursuit of wealth. It will be very lonely at the top of the ladder success if you do not have anyone to share your success with.

6. Plan For Tomorrow

Make plans for the next day. Prioritize your task. Make a list of those that are critical to least important. Assess your day if you had accomplished your entire task, and if you had not, what prevented you from achieving that task. If it is possible, you should exercise in the evenings too.

Say goodbye to the world of work with whatever relaxation techniques you have and settle in for a healthy prosperous future.

Chapter 7

Evening Success Rituals

Now I will share with you the evening success rituals for going to bed every night feeling fulfilled with a big smile on your face! These rituals are the follow-up to your morning rituals to reflect and celebrate after your day's activities.

While morning rituals are highly encouraged to be incorporated into everyone's daily routine, the evening rituals are equally as important to get the most out of your day. After all, there is no point to start off a race full of energy but no idea how to end it.

So, I don't want you to miss this crucial part to inspire your success and celebrate it. You may be consistently crushing your goals one after another, but unless you take the time to celebrate every victory in your life, then you're definitely not getting the most out of your day and missing out on a lot of magic moments and sense of fulfillment that you should be experiencing at this moment.

Here are the Evening Success Rituals that I highly recommend incorporating into your evening routine:

1. Empowering Evening Questions

At the beginning of the Evening Success Rituals, the main focus is to reflect your day. And the best way to reflect is to ask powerful questions, not just any other questions that beat yourself up. I called these powerful questions "Empowering Evening Questions", designed to help you reflect on your entire day and come up with constructive ideas to shape a better tomorrow.

So the first thing you should do is to find a quiet place, where you won't be easily disturbed and distracted for a set amount of time in order to go deep in your daily reflection.

The questions you ask determine what you focus on. That's the reason why the type of questions you ask yourself is extremely important. Ask a lousy question, and you will feel lousy; Ask a good question, and you will feel amazing!

For example, how you feel about 'Today' is ultimately based on the Good or Bad you focused on.

Let me ask you this... What were the things that happened today that you can feel good about?

I'd bet you can come up with a long list of things! It could be the fact that you're alive, or you went for a walk, or you had a wonderful time with your loved ones, or you had done a good deed, had a fantastic dinner, crossed off ONE stuff on your to-do list... Whatever it is, you can always find something to feel good about every single day.

Now let me ask you again... What were the things that happened today that you feel awful about?

Again, I'd bet you can list out a lot of things. It could be that you procrastinated on your tasks, ate some nasty junk food, failed to pick up that call, skipped the gym, said some awful things to people you care for, and so on... Ultimately, how'd you feel after answering this question? Of course, AWFUL!

The fact is, there is always Good and Bad in each day, and what you ask yourself decides what you'll focus on each night before hitting the sack. What you focus on determine how you feel about that particular day.

Since there is always Good and Bad, why not be proactive and decide that you only want to acknowledge the Good that happened that day? Since you can decide how you're going to feel at the end of the day, why not choose to feel good instead of bad?

Guess what happens if you constantly ask yourself Empowering Evening Questions? Every day will be an awesome day for you, and you'll always feel like a rockstar! Now, think of the level of accomplishments, productivity, and fulfillment you'll experience every day... I'll let you know about mine - Phenomenal! In fact, there is no such thing as a bad day.

It all starts with your focus, and these Empowering Evening Questions will help you to do just that.

And here's a list of questions that I ask myself every evening:

What was fantastic about today? What did I learn today? What am I grateful for today?

What was my biggest accomplishment for today? What would

make today great?

Don't just write down all your answers, try to FEEL the emotions and energy coursing through your veins as you read out your answers out loud.

Do this with level 10 intensity - move, gesture and smile widely as you answer them. Allow yourself to feel proud, excited, happy, loved, appreciated, etc... Trust me, you'll be amazed by what this simple exercise can do to your physical and emotional well-being. The more emotional intensity you put into this exercise, the more juice you'll get from the Empowering Evening Questions exercise.

2. Seizing Your Magic Moments

A life worth living is a worth life recording. - Jim Rohn

After you've gone through the Empowering Evening Questions exercise, you'll be in an incredible state. But you don't want to stop right there. You should take this opportunity to seize these emotions and feelings by journaling all your successes, accomplishments and magic moments. Otherwise, they'd be forgotten.

So take out a journal and write down everything that happened on that day. List down everything that you had done and all the powerful moments that you want to remember later on.

Time passes by so fast, and we easily forget to really take in and appreciate the little things. At the end of your life, you won't be able to remember everything, but only certain moments. So I want to encourage you to take your time and capture all your successes and magic moments into your journal.

One day, when you're feeling down and see no hope in life, you have a journal to go back to and remind yourself of all the magic moments that you once had and realize that your life is actually more incredible than you think. By journalling your magic moments, you'll be aware of what you were doing with your time and celebrate your victory.

3. Celebrate

Last but not least, CELEBRATE! Celebrate your day to your heart content, you deserve it! This is a powerful way to reinforce yourself positively.

Don't beat yourself up for things you didn't do, tasks you procrastinated, the food you shouldn't eat, etc... Because that's what most people do, which prompts them to feel awful and guilty about themselves.

To make things worse, they repeat this process every day, and they end up in a downward spiral that sets themselves up for more failures. Why bring so much pain in your life when there is so many Good that happens every day? Why not start recognizing and celebrating all the Good that happened that day?

What gets rewarded, gets repeated.

When you celebrate your victory often, you'll invite more amazing things into your life. And soon, you'll be conditioned to notice the Good in every little thing that happens in your life. And soon, you'll develop powerful habits such as gratitude, consistency, tenacity, and self-discipline.

So how do you celebrate?

You really don't have to complicate things. Celebrating means giving yourself pleasure. It could be as simple as patting yourself on the back and say to yourself 'Good Job!', treat yourself a whole-hearty meal, giving thanks, listening to your favorite music, or meditating with gratitude.

The key is to give yourself pleasure. Often times, we wait for others to praise, acknowledge, and reward us in order to feel happy, appreciated, and fulfilled. Why not be proactive and reward yourself when you can choose to be happy right now?

Conclusion

Do not give up on your dreams. It might take time for you to achieve your goals, but with the power that is embedded in your mind, you can conquer the world one day at a time. Never let procrastination cripple your progress. Do not let failure deter you; learn whatever lesson that comes with failing, then restart your journey.

The more you use your skills, you will discover other hidden treasures of ability that were buried in you. I can guarantee that you will be astonished at the things that you can do. Your talent can take you to places you have not even started to imagine about. The hard work and the sacrifices you make to attain success will be worth it. In fact, when you start your journey to success, each challenge you overcome will become a distant memory because the rewards will outweigh the struggles.

 Remember, success is a lifestyle, one that a taste of it is very addictive. You can have your taste of success too. I might not know your name or where you are from.

I might not know what you have been through or what you are going through now. However, I know that you have something within you, something that sets you apart from the rest of the individuals in your line of work. You need to find that part of your skill because it is your key to the door of success. No one in the world can do it for you; this is something you have to do on your own.

I believe the fact that you have purchased this book is because that key, which is a part of your skill, has been nudging you. It is telling you that you can do this, you have what it takes. Do not be afraid. All it takes are some small steps, and the small steps will one day be a very long journey, a journey of no regrets because you tried and had achieved.

Everything in life is a choice; the only thing we do not have a choice about is when we will die.

If you have created doubt within yourself at this moment, thinking that you do not have the money to invest in your plans, then the money is not hindering you from achieving your goals, only you are preventing yourself from progressing. Watch your inner thoughts; they will influence what you do. Speak positive words to yourself every day. You will have many options, but never choose to quit, no matter how bad things get.

Work on you, self-education is a powerful tool. Utilize technology. Make some connection with people, who are successful in your field, sell them your plans. Describe your goals with such passion that they have to listen to you.

Prepare yourself for the "No's," it is just a part of your learning experience on your journey. Do not get mad at those who will reject your plans. You cannot blame them for not understanding the greatness that lies within you. Most of the individuals who will tell you, "No" now, will one day plead with you to join their team.

Keep a firm hold on your spirituality; it can ground you, bring you clarity, and motivate you to understand your inner self. Finding your place in the universe and with spirituality does not need to be religiously based. Spirituality is a state of consciousness that enables you to specify your desires and future with a clear mind and relaxed body.

So dear reader, what will be your choice?

I believe you will take your first small step to success, by conquering your fear and misery because you are going to build your own success rituals as soon as you finish reading this book.

Thank you for reading this book, and I am looking forward to seeing you at the top of the ladder of success. Good Luck!

Lightning Source UK Ltd.
Milton Keynes UK
UKHW020206141220
375014UK00004B/466